The True Life

The True Life

Alain Badiou

Translated by Susan Spitzer

polity

First published in French as *La vraie vie* © Librairie Arthème Fayard, 2016

This English edition © Polity Press, 2017
Reprinted 2017 (twice)

Polity Press
65 Bridge Street
Cambridge CB2 1UR, UK

Polity Press
350 Main Street
Malden, MA 02148, USA

ISBN-13: 978-1-5095-1488-5
ISBN-13: 978-1-5095-1489-2 (pb)

A catalogue record for this book is available from the British Library.

Library of Congress Cataloging-in-Publication Data

Names: Badiou, Alain, author.
Title: The true life : a plea for corrupting the young / Alain Badiou.
Other titles: Vaie vie. English
Description: Malden, MA : Polity, 2017. | Includes bibliographical references and index.
Identifiers: LCCN 2016038450 (print) | LCCN 2016047845 (ebook) | ISBN 9781509514885 (hardback) | ISBN 9781509514892 (pbk.) | ISBN 9781509514915 (Mobi) | ISBN 9781509514922 (Epub)
Subjects: LCSH: Youth--Social aspects. | Lifestyles. | Corruption.
Classification: LCC HQ796 .B235 2017 (print) | LCC HQ796 (ebook) | DDC 305.235--dc23
LC record available at https://lccn.loc.gov/2016038450

Typeset in 12.5 on 15 pt Adobe Garamond by Servis Filmsetting Ltd, Stockport, Cheshire
Printed and bound in the United States by LSC Communications

For further information on Polity, visit our website: politybooks.com

Contents

v

Note

This book is based on lectures, all of which were intended mainly for young people and were delivered in a variety of places, including high schools, but also other institutions, both in France and abroad (in Belgium and Greece in particular), as well as in my seminar. One of them (the second chapter of this book) has already been published as an Afterword to *Anthropologie de la guerre*, a collection of Freud's essays on war (Fayard, 2010). What I am offering here is the latest version of these lectures, with the idea of starting a discussion between contemporary youth and philosophy about what the true life is – in general, first of all, and then depending on whether one is a girl or a boy.

To be young, today: sense and nonsense

Let's start with the realities: I'm 79 years old. So why on earth should I concern myself with speaking about youth? And why should I, in addition, care about speaking about it to young people themselves? Aren't they the ones who should speak about their own experience as young people? Am I here to give lessons of wisdom, like an old man who knows life's dangers and teaches the young to be careful, keep quiet, and just leave the world the way it is?

You'll perhaps see, or I hope you will, that it's quite the opposite, that I'm speaking to young people about what life has to offer, about why it is absolutely necessary to change the world, about why, precisely for that reason, risks must be taken.

I'm going to begin pretty far back, however, with a famous episode concerning philosophy. Socrates, the father of all philosophers, was condemned to death on charges of "corrupting youth." The very first reception of philosophy on record was in the form of a very serious accusation: the philosopher corrupts youth. So, if I were to adopt that view, I would simply say: my aim is to corrupt youth.

But what did "corrupt" mean, including in the minds of the judges who condemned Socrates to death on charges of corrupting youth? It couldn't be "corruption" in a sense related to money. It wasn't a "scandal" in the sense of the ones you read about in the press today, where people have gotten rich by exploiting their positions in one institution of the State or another. That was certainly not what Socrates' judges accused him of. On the contrary, let's not forget that one of the criticisms Socrates leveled against his rivals, the so-called sophists, was precisely that they got paid. He, on the other hand, corrupted youth for free, so to speak, with his revolutionary lessons, while the sophists were paid handsomely for the lessons they gave, which were lessons of opportunism. "Corrupting youth," as regards

Socrates, was therefore certainly not a matter of money.

Nor was it a matter of moral corruption, let alone one of those sorts of sexual scandals that you also read about in the press. On the contrary, Socrates, or Plato relating – or making up? – Socrates' point of view, had a particularly sublime conception of love, a conception that didn't separate love from sex but gradually detached it from it for the sake of a sort of subjective ascension. To be sure, this ascension could, and even should, begin through contact with beautiful bodies. But such contact couldn't be reduced to mere sexual excitation, because it was the material basis for accessing what Socrates called the idea of the Beautiful. And so love was ultimately the birth of a new thinking, which arose not from sex alone but from what could be called sexual love-subjected-to-thought. And this love-thought was a part of intellectual and spiritual self-construction.

Ultimately, the corruption of youth by a philosopher is a question neither of money nor of pleasure. Might it then be a question of corruption through power? Sex, money, and power are a triad of sorts, the triad of corruption. To say that Socrates corrupted youth would be to say that he took advantage of his seductive speech to gain power. The philosopher supposedly used young people for the purpose of gaining power or authority. The young people existed to serve his ambition. So there was supposedly corruption of youth in the sense that their naïveté was integrated into what one could call, with Nietzsche, the will to power.

But once again I would say: "*Au contraire!*" Socrates, as seen by Plato, explicitly denounces the corrupting nature of power. It is power that corrupts, not the philosopher. In Plato's work there is a scathing critique of tyranny, of the desire for power, that cannot be improved upon and is in a way the last word on the subject. There is even the opposite conviction: what the philosopher can contribute to politics is not at all the will to power, but disinterestedness.

So you see that we end up with a conception of philosophy completely foreign to ambition and competition for power.

In this connection, I'd like to read you a passage from Plato's *Republic* in the rather unusual translation I did of it. You can find it, if you so desire, in paperback. On the cover there's the following information: "Alain Badiou" (the author's name) and, below it, "*Plato's* Republic" (the title of the book). So it's not clear who wrote the book: Plato? Badiou? Or perhaps Socrates, who is said never to have written anything? It's an arrogant title, I admit. But the result is perhaps a livelier book, one that's more accessible for a young person today than a strict translation of Plato's text might be.

What I'm going to read you takes place when Plato asks himself the following question: What exactly is the relationship between power and philosophy, between political power and philosophy? We can thus appreciate the importance he attaches to disinterestedness in politics.

Socrates is speaking to two interlocutors, two young people, in fact, and that's why we're not getting off topic here. In Plato's original version, they are two boys, Glaucon and Adeimantus. In my obviously more modern version, there's a boy, Glaucon, and a girl, Amantha. Including girls on the same basis as boys is the least you can do today if you're speaking about young people, or to them. Here is the dialogue:

Socrates: If we can come up with a much better life
    for those whose turn has come to be responsible for

5

a certain share of power than the one offered them by that power, then we'll have the potential for a true political community, because then the only people who will come to power are the ones for whom wealth isn't measured in money but rather in what's required for happiness: the true life, full of sublime thoughts. If, however, people hungry for personal advantage, people who are sure that power always favors the existence and expansion of private property, rush into public affairs, then no true political community will be possible. People like that always fight ferociously with one another for power, and a war of that sort, combining private passions and public power, destroys not only the rivals for the top positions but the country as a whole.

Glaucon: What a hideous spectacle!

Socrates: But tell me, do you know of any life that can inspire contempt for power and the State?

Amantha: Of course! The life of the true philosopher, the life of Socrates!

Socrates [*delighted*]**:** Let's not get carried away. Let's assume that people who are in love with power should never be in power, because if they were, we'd have nothing but war between the rivals for power. That's why it's necessary for that enormous

mass of people whom I unhesitatingly call philosophers to devote themselves, each in turn, to
guarding the political community: selfless people,
who are instinctively aware of what public service
can be but who know that there are many other
rewards besides the ones you can get from fre-
quenting government offices, and that there's a life
that's a lot better than the life of political leaders.

Amantha [*in a murmur*]: The true life.

Socrates: The true life. Which is never absent. Or
never entirely.[1]

So there you have it. Philosophy's subject
matter is the true life. What is a true life? That is
the philosopher's sole question. And so, if there
is corruption of youth, it's not for the sake of
money, pleasure, or power but to show the young
that there is something better than all those things:
the true life. Something worthwhile, something
worth living for, that far outstrips money, pleasure, and power.

The "true life," let's not forget, is a phrase of
Rimbaud's. Now *there* was a true poet of youth:
Rimbaud. Someone who made poetry out of his

1 Alain Badiou, *Plato's* Republic, tr. Susan Spitzer (New
York: Columbia University Press, 2012), 321.

7

whole experience of life as it was beginning. It was he who, in a moment of despair, wrote heartbreakingly: "The true life is absent."

What philosophy teaches us, or at any rate tries to teach us, is that, although the true life isn't always present, it is never completely absent either. That the true life is present to some extent is what the philosopher tries to show. And he corrupts the young in that he attempts to show them that there is a false life, a devastated life, which is a life conceived of and lived as a fierce struggle for power and money. A life reduced in every possible way to the pure and simple gratification of immediate impulses.

Basically, says Socrates – and I'm just following him for now – to attain the true life we have to struggle against prejudices, preconceived ideas, blind obedience, arbitrary customs, and unrestricted competition. Essentially, to corrupt youth means only one thing: to try to ensure that young people don't go down the paths already mapped out, that they are not just condemned to obey social customs, that they can create something new, propose a different direction as regards the true life.

When all is said and done, I think the starting

point is Socrates' belief that young people have two inner enemies. It is these inner enemies that threaten to turn them away from the true life and keep them from recognizing the potential for the true life in themselves.

The first enemy is what could be called the passion for immediate life, for amusement, pleasure, the moment, some song or other, a fling, a joint, or some stupid game. All of that exists; Socrates doesn't try to deny it. But when it all builds up, when it's carried to its extreme, when that passion produces a life that is lived from one day to the next, a life dependent on the immediacy of time, a life in which the future is invisible or at any rate totally obscure, then what you get is a kind of nihilism, a kind of conception of life with no unified meaning – a life devoid of meaning and consequently unable to go on as a true life. What is called "life" in that case is a period of time divided into more or less good and more or less bad moments, and, in the end, having the most good-enough moments possible – that and that alone – is all that can be hoped for from life.

Ultimately, this conception shatters the idea of life itself, breaks it up, and that's why this vision of life is also a vision of death. This is a profound idea explicitly expounded by Plato: when life is subject in this way to temporal immediacy, it falls apart by itself, dissipates, is no longer recognizable to itself, no longer tied to a stable meaning. Using Freudian and psychoanalytic terminology, which Plato often anticipated in many respects, we could say that this vision of life is one in which the life drive is secretly inhabited by the death drive. At an unconscious level, death takes hold of life, undermining it and detaching it from its potential meaning. This is young people's first inner enemy, because they inevitably go through this experience. They have to undergo the wrenching experience of the deathly power of the immediate. Philosophy's aim is not to deny this living experience of inner death but to overcome it.

On the other hand, the second inner threat for a young person is seemingly the opposite: the passion for success, the idea of becoming someone rich, powerful, and well established. Not the idea of consuming oneself in immediate life but, on the contrary, of obtaining a good position in the existing social order. Life then becomes the sum total of tactics for becoming well established, even it means you have to be better than everyone else at submitting to the existing order so as to succeed in it. This is not the regime of instant gratification of pleasure; it's that of the well-conceived, highly effective plan. Your good education begins right from pre-school, and you go on to one of the best, carefully chosen middle schools. You end up in a high school like Henri IV or Louis-le-Grand, in particular – from which I myself, incidentally, graduated. And you continue, if possible, along the same path: *grandes écoles*, boards of directors, high finance, mass media, government ministries, trade boards, start-ups valued at billions on the stock market, and so on.

Basically, when you're young, you're faced, often without being clearly aware of it, with two possible life directions, which are sometimes overlapping and contradictory. I could sum up these two temptations like this: either the passion for burning up your life or the passion for building it. Burning it up means the nihilistic cult of the immediate, which, by the way, may very well be the cult of pure revolt, insurrection, insubordination, rebellion, new, dazzling but short-lived forms of collective life, such as the occupations of public squares for a few weeks. But as we see, as we know, there is no lasting effect, no construction, no organized control of time in any of that. You march under the slogan "No future." And if, on the contrary, you orient your life toward future fulfillment, success, money, social status, a well-paying career, a quiet family life, and vacations in the South Sea isles, the result will be a conservative cult of the existing power structure, since you'll arrange your life within it in the best possible way.

These are the two alternatives that are always present in the simple fact of being young, of having to begin, and therefore to orient, one's life: to burn up or to build. Or both, but doing both is not so easy. It would mean building a fire, and the fire burns and blazes, the fire glows, it warms and illuminates moments of life. However, it destroys rather than builds.

It is because there are these two conflicting passions that there have been – for a long time, not just now – such conflicting opinions about youth. Widely differing opinions, ranging from the idea that youth is a wonderful time of life to the idea that it's a terrible time of life.

Both these versions have always existed in literature. There is indeed something unique about youth, whatever the historical era, and I think it is precisely this conflict between the passions, with two basic passions: the desire for a life consumed by its own intensity, and the desire for a life that you build stone by stone in order to have a comfortable house in the city.

Let me quote a few of these opinions for you. Let's take, for example, two lines by the Hugo of *The Legend of the Ages*, from the famous poem "Boaz Asleep":

Our mornings rise triumphantly in youth,
Day comes from darkness like a victory . . .[2]

Youth is a triumph, Hugo says, evoking moreover, at once discreetly and forcefully, the mornings of lovemaking, of sensual victory.

But let's take Paul Nizan now, from the beginning of his book *Aden Arabie*: "I was twenty, I won't let anyone say those are the best years of your life."[3]

Youth, Nizan tells us, is in any case not the

2 *Selected Poems of Victor Hugo: A Bilingual Edition*, tr. E. H. Blackmore and A. M. Blackmore (Chicago: University of Chicago Press, 2001), 339.
3 Paul Nizan, *Aden Arabie*, tr. Joan Pinkham (New York: Columbia University Press, 1987), 59.

best part of life. So, is youth a triumph, a triumph of life? Or an uncertain and rather painful time, because it is a conflictual time, a time of confusion?

This conflict in all its force can be found in many writers, and particularly poets. It may, for example, be the central theme of Rimbaud's whole body of work. Rimbaud is interesting because, I repeat, he is the great poet of youth. He is youth incarnate in poetry. But Rimbaud holds both opinions; he says both things at once: youth is a wonderful figure, and youth is a figure that must absolutely be relegated to the past. Let's compare two literally opposite aspects of that autobiographical prose poem *A Season in Hell.*

At the beginning of the poem, in the first sentence, we find:

> Once, if I remember well, my life was a feast where all hearts opened and all wines flowed.[4]

This "once" refers to the seventeen-year-old Rimbaud, as seen by the twenty-year-old

---

4 *A Season in Hell and The Drunken Boat*, tr. Louise Varese (New York: New Directions, 1961), 3. Subsequent references to this edition will appear in parentheses in the text.

Rimbaud. So it's about a life consumed at lightning speed but that sees its beginning as a time of feasts, love, and intoxication.

Later, toward the end of the text, he will say, as if he were an old man woefully recalling the now-vanished halcyon days of youth:

> Had I not *once* a lovely youth, heroic, fabulous, to be written on sheets of gold. . . ! ("Morning," 81)

But the Rimbaud of this poignant lament, this nostalgic old man who is scarcely twenty, is already caught up in the other passion, the sensible construction of life, and he writes the following, which is like a renunciation of the deathly power of impulses, of narcissistic self-relation, and of constant immorality:

> I! I who called myself angel or seer, exempt from all morality, I am returned to the soil with a duty to seek and rough reality to embrace
>
> ("Adieu," 87)

And at the very end, this theme returns, connected with the renunciation of poetry itself:

> No hymns: hold the ground gained. Arduous night! The dried blood smokes on my face and I

have nothing behind me but that horrible bush! . . .
Spiritual combat is as brutal as the battle of men: but
the vision of justice is the pleasure of God alone.

Meanwhile, this is the vigil. Welcome then, all the
influx of vigor and real tenderness. And in the dawn,
armed with an ardent patience, we shall enter mag-
nificent cities.

(89)

You see: at the beginning, the passion for a
life burned-up, impetuous heroism, poetry and
feasts; and at the end, no more hymns, which
means: no more poems. There is a conversion to
the rough necessity of duty, of the well-built life.
And what is needed, quite contrary to what pre-
vailed over his misspent youth, is patience, ardent
patience. In only three years, Rimbaud ran the
whole gamut of youth's two possible directions:
the absolute rule of immediacy and its pleasures,
or the rough patience required by the duty to
succeed. He had been an itinerant poet, and he
would become a colonial arms dealer.

I will now turn to a question that, truth be
told, I ask young people at least as much as I ask
myself. On what scales can youth be weighed
today? Since we know that diametrically opposed

16

opinions have been expressed, what would we say today? What would we record as the result of a weighing of the two terms of the contradiction constitutive of youth? Toward which side would the scales tip?

There are positive features that seem to characterize contemporary youth and ought to make it different from previous generations of youth. Indeed, it could be argued that, for a number of reasons, young people have greater freedom of action today than in the past, both to burn up their lives and to build them. Simply put, it seems as though the most common feature of youth, at least in our world, the world known as the West, is that it is a freer youth.

First of all, it is a youth that is no longer subjected to a harsh initiation. Initiation rites, which were often severe, are no longer imposed to mark the passage from youth to adulthood. Such an initiation existed for many centuries and was a very important part of human history. For the tens of thousands of years of the existence of man, the mammal, the featherless biped, there were always initiation rites – specific, socially established passages between youth and adulthood. These might have been bodily markings, daunting physical and moral tests, or activities that were prohibited before and permitted afterwards. And all these things indicated that "young person" meant "someone who has not yet been initiated." There was a restrictive, negative definition of youth. "To be young" was above all "not to be an adult yet."

I think that this frame of mind, these symbolic customs, lasted up until not all that long ago. Let's assume for a moment that my age, even though advanced, is hardly anything when measured against the scale of the human animal's whole historical existence. So I can say that my youth doesn't date back to very long ago. And yet it's absolutely clear that, still during my youth, there was a rite of initiation for males, in the guise of military service. And there was one for females, in marriage. A young man was considered an adult when he had done his military service, and a young woman was considered an adult when she got married. Today, these last two vestiges of initiation are no more than memories for grandparents. So it can be said that youth escapes the issue of initiation.

The second feature I would highlight is that there is less, infinitely less, value placed on old age. In traditional society, the elders were always the ones in charge; they were valued as such, naturally to the detriment of the young people. Wisdom was on the side of long experience, advanced age, old age. Now, that valorization has disappeared in favor of its opposite: the valorization of youth. This is what has been called "the cult of youth." The cult of youth is like a reversal of the old cult of the wise elders. I mean this on a theoretical, or rather ideological, level, because power is still largely concentrated in the hands of adults and even the aging. But the cult of youth, as an ideology, as a theme of commercial advertising, permeates society, which takes the young as its model. As Plato, moreover, predicted about democratic societies, we have the impression that it's the old who want to stay young at all costs, rather than the young who want to become adults. The cult of youth is the tendency to cling as tightly as possible to youth, beginning with bodily youth, rather than to assume the wisdom of age as something superior. That's why "staying in shape" is the imperative of the aging. Constant jogging and tennis, fitness, plastic surgery – whatever it takes. You've got to be young and stay young. Old people in sweats run in the park, taking their blood pressure as they go along. So there's a serious problem for the aging, for those who, even if they *have* gone running in the park, are bound to grow old and die – in other words, everyone. But that's another matter.

There may also be, at least on the face of it, less internal differentiation, less of a class difference – let's not mince words – among the young themselves. You don't have to go very far back in the past to see this. Consider that, in my youth, only about 10 percent of a given age group took the *bac* [the high school exit exam]. And now, in only a matter of a few decades, 60 to 70 percent do. In my youth, a real educational gulf separated us from the kids who hadn't taken the *bac*, or even – and they were the vast majority – those who hadn't gone to high school, the kids who stopped going to school at around 11 or 12 years old, at what was called the *certificat d'études*, which meant that you knew how to read and write, that you knew how to count, and that you could thus become a skilled worker in the big cities. You also knew that our ancestors were the Gauls, and you could therefore die for your country in the trenches of World War I, or even die (I'm talking about 1954–62 – only yesterday, in other words) hunting down the "towelheads" in Algeria, in the Aurès Mountains. This double destiny – working-class and military – sufficed for 90 percent of the young men. The rest, the elite, the 10 percent, continued their education for at least another seven years, and thus climbed the ladder of social prestige.

Back in the days that in fact nearly coincided with those of my youth, it was almost as if there were two different societies within society, or at any rate two different types of youth. The youth of those whose education lasted a long time was a different world from the youth of those whose education didn't and who were in the overwhelming majority.

It may well be that, today, this class gulf between two different types of youth, which is obviously less visible, nevertheless continues to exist in other guises, including, in particular, origin, place of residence, customs, religion, and even habituses such as clothing, consumption, and the conception of immediate life. It is possibly an even deeper – though less pronounced, less formal, less apparent – gulf. However, that, too, is another matter.

Given everything I've just mentioned, it can

be argued that being young is no longer subject to the social demarcation between young people and adults in the guise of initiation, and that the transition from youth to adulthood is therefore smoother. It can also be agreed that youth is a little more homogeneous in terms of its rites and customs – its "culture," in a word. Lastly, it can be said that the spiritual cult of old age has reversed into a materialistic cult of eternal youth.

To sum up, it could be said that it's not so bad to be young today, it's actually a stroke of luck. It was worse before; it was a constraint. It could be said that the features of contemporary youth are largely those of a new freedom and that the young are therefore lucky to be young, whereas it's tough luck to be old. The wind has shifted.

Well, it's not as simple as all that.

To begin with, the fact that there's no initiation is a double-edged sword. On the one hand, it subjects the young to a sort of endless adolescence, hence to the impossibility of dealing with the passions I mentioned, of controlling those passions, and this in turn leads to what could be called (it's the same thing, but the other way around) a puerilization of adults. An infantilization. Young people can remain young indefinitely because there is no specific demarcation, which means that adulthood is both continually and partially an extension of childhood. This infantilization of adults could be said to be directly linked to the influence of the market, because life, in our society, is to some extent the possibility of buying. Buying what? Toys, ultimately – big toys, things that we like and that impress other people. And contemporary society orders us to buy these things, to want to be able to buy as many of them as possible. Now, the idea of buying things, of playing with new things – new cars, brand-name shoes, enormous TVs, apartments with a southern exposure, gold-plated smartphones, vacations in Croatia, imitation Persian carpets, all that sort of thing – is typical of a child's or a teenager's desires. When it also becomes something at work in adults, even if only partially, there is no longer any symbolic boundary between being young and being an adult. It's a sort of smooth continuity. The adult becomes someone who's a little better able than the young person to afford to buy big toys. The difference is more quantitative than qualitative. So, between young people's adolescence and the general and infantilizing submission to the law of buying, with subjects who all appear before the glittering goods on the global marketplace, the upshot is a sort of drifting of youth. Back in the days when initiation existed, youth was stationary, but now it is adrift; it doesn't know what its borders or boundaries are. It is both separate and indistinguishable from adulthood, and this state of being adrift is also what I'd call disorientation.

What about the second argument in youth's favor, namely the fact that old age is no longer valued? Well, this has significantly increased the fear of youth, which sticks to its exclusive valorization like its shadow. This fear of youth, of working-class youth in particular, is very typical of our society. And there's nothing to counterbalance it any more. In the past, there was a fear of youth in the sense that old age, the wisdom passed down from the older generation, was supposed to contain or control it, impose identities and limits on it. But today there is something far more ominous, which is the fear of youth's disorientation. People are afraid of youth precisely because they're not sure what it is or what it is capable of being, because it is internal to the adult world itself and, at the same time, not completely internal to it; it is other without being other. The sheer number of repressive laws, police actions, frivolous investigations, and procedures explicitly intended to deal with this fear of youth is a very significant symptom. It needs to be assessed, and young people should assess it. They live in a society that glorifies youth and fears it at the same time, no doubt about it. And, as a result of this balance between the two, our society fails to deal with the problem of its own youth. Or, more precisely, a very large proportion of the youth in our cities is now regarded as a major problem. And when, as is the case today, society is unable to provide work for these young people, the problems become really serious, because having a job was in a way the last kind of initiation. It was then that adult life seemed to begin. Even this occurs much later – is very delayed – nowadays. And what remains is the youth in the housing projects as a disoriented, dangerous class.

As for the third argument, namely that there is a smaller cultural or educational gap between middle-class and working-class youth than there was 50 years ago, it's important to understand that other differences, as I mentioned, have appeared. Differences in origin, identity, attire, place of residence, religion, and so on. I'd say that a gulf has opened up within an apparently undivided youth. Previously, up until the 1980s and thereafter, youth was divided in two. Young people who were destined for high-ranking positions were separated early on from those who were to remain workers or farmers. There were two worlds. Now the world looks more like one world. But the idea that within this one world there are serious, insurmountable differences is gradually taking hold. Student demonstrations have become completely separate from the violent riots of the youth in the housing projects. Even though categorically denied where school is concerned, the division of youth is reproduced in disorientation and mistrust.

Let's call "the world of tradition" the age-old world of strict authoritarian control by the social group over its youth: a coded, regulated, symbolized form of authority that closely supervised everything relating to the activity and the very few rights of boys and, to an even greater extent, girls. I think it's safe to say that young people's obvious new freedoms prove that we're not in the world of tradition anymore. But it's also clear that not being in it anymore raises problems, most of which are still not resolved – where the young are concerned any more than where the old are concerned. The former are adrift and inspire fear, while the latter are devalued and placed in institutions, with their only fate being to die "in peace."

So let me propose a militant idea. It would be very reasonable to organize a huge demonstration for an alliance of the young and the old, directed against today's adults, in fact. The most rebellious of the under-30-year-olds and the toughest of the over-60-year-olds against the well-established 40- and 50-year-olds. The young people would say they're fed up with being adrift, disoriented, and endlessly lacking any sign of their positive existence. They'd also say that it's wrong for the adults to pretend that they're eternally young. The old folks would say that they're fed up with paying for their devaluation, for being stripped out of the traditional image of the wise elder, by being put out to pasture, moved into nursing homes where they're left to die, and with their total lack of social visibility. This joint demonstration would be something very new and very important! Incidentally, over the course of my many trips throughout the world I've seen a lot of conferences, a lot of situations, where the audience was composed of a small core of old veterans, old survivors like myself of the big battles of the sixties and seventies, and loads of young people who'd come to see whether the philosopher had anything to say about the orientation of their lives and the possibility of a true life. So all over the world I've seen the lineaments of the alliance I'm talking to you about. Just as in leap-frog, young people today seem to need to jump over the dominant age group, the one that goes roughly from 35 to 65, in order to form with the little core group of old rebels – the unresigned – an alliance of disoriented youth and old veterans of life. Together, we would demand that the path of the true life be opened up.

While waiting for this glorious demonstration to happen, I would say that young people are on the brink of a new world, a world that will no longer be the age-old world of tradition. Not every generation is on the brink of a new world; it's a situation unique to the young people I'm specifically speaking to here.

You are living at a time of crisis in societies that is shaking off and destroying the last vestiges of tradition. And we don't really know what the positive side of this destruction or negation is. We know that it unquestionably leads to a kind of freedom. But that freedom is above all the absence of certain taboos. It is a negative, consumerist freedom condemned to the constant variation of commodities, fashions, and opinions. It sets no direction for a new idea of the true life. And at the same time, where young people are concerned, it creates disorientation and fear, and it is unclear how society will cope with this, because it only counters it with the false life of competition and material success. Determining what a creative, positive freedom might be will be the task of the new world to come.

Actually, the issue we all need to address is this: modernity is the abandonment of tradition. It is the end of the old world of castes, nobilities, hereditary monarchs, religious obligation, initiations of the young, the subjugation of women, the rigid, formal, established, symbolically very stark separation between the powerful few and the masses of disdained, hard-working farmers, workers, and migrants. Nothing can reverse this irresistible movement, no doubt begun in the West during the Renaissance; consolidated ideologically by the Enlightenment in the eighteenth century; embodied since then in the unprecedented development of production technologies and the ongoing refinement of the means of calculation, circulation, and communication; and subjected, from the nineteenth century on, to the political struggle between globalizing capitalism and the collectivist, communist idea, with its experiments, its terrible failures, and its dogged reconstructions. A struggle that was, and still is, about the form and consequences of modernity, regarded as the abandonment of tradition.

Perhaps the most striking point, and in any case the one we'll be focusing on here, is that this abandonment of the world of tradition – this veritable tornado overtaking humanity, which in barely three centuries has swept away forms of organization that had lasted for thousands of years – is creating a subjective crisis, the causes and extent of which we are seeing today and one of whose most glaring aspects is the extreme and increasing difficulty experienced by young people in finding their place in the new world.

That's what the real crisis is. Everybody talks about "the crisis" today. People sometimes think it's the crisis of modern finance capitalism. But it's not! Not at all! Capitalism is expanding rapidly all over the world, and its natural mode of development has always included crises and wars, means as brutal as they are necessary for streamlining the forms of competition and consolidating the position of the winners – those who succeed, by bankrupting all the others, in concentrating in their own hands the largest possible amount of the available capital.

Let's review the current situation. As Mao Zedong used to say, we should always "have the figures in mind." Today, 10% of the world population own 86% of the available capital. 1% own 46% of that capital. And 50% of the world population own exactly nothing, 0%. It is easy to see why the 10% who own practically everything don't want to be lumped together with those who have nothing, or even with the less prosperous of those who share between them the scant remaining 14%. What's more, many of those who share that 14% are very roughly split between passive resentment and a ferocious desire to hold on to what they've got, in particular by the support they give, with racism and nationalism playing their parts, to the countless repressive barriers against the terrible "threat" they perceive in the 50% who have nothing.

All this, incidentally, means that the supposedly unifying slogan of the Occupy Wall Street movement, "We are the 99%," was totally meaningless. The participants in the movement, full of good will that they should be commended for, were probably for the most part young people from families somewhere "in the middle," neither truly poor nor really rich – the middle class, in a word, which is hyped as loving democracy, as being a pillar of democracy. But the truth is, the affluent West is full of people from that "middle," that middle class, who, even though they're not in the 1% of the wealthy elite or in the 10% of well-off property owners, nevertheless fear the 50% of complete have-nots, and, clinging to the tiny 14% of resources that they share among themselves, provide globalized capitalism with the petit-bourgeois troop of supporters without which the "democratic" oasis would have no chance of surviving. Far from being "the 99%," even symbolically, the brave young people of the Occupy Wall Street movement amounted, even in terms of their own original group, to no more than a small number of people, whose fate was to fade away.

Unless, of course, they forged a very serious bond with the real masses of those who have nothing, or really not much, unless they established a political alliance between the people in the 14%, the intellectuals in particular, and those in the 50%. Such a political strategy is feasible: it was attempted, with some significant local successes, in France in the sixties and seventies under the banner of Maoism; in the US, during the same period, with less fanfare, by the Weathermen; and a few years ago by the Occupy movements, not on Wall Street but in Tunis and Cairo, and even in Oakland, where there were at least the beginnings of a real connection with the dockworkers. Everything, absolutely everything, depends on the definitive revival of this alliance and its political organization on a worldwide scale.

However, in the extremely weak state of such a movement, the objective, measurable outcome of the abandonment of tradition – since it is occurring within the globalized formalism of capitalism – is what I just said about it: a tiny oligarchy lays down the law to an overwhelming majority of people who are just barely surviving, and to Westernized – i.e., vassalized and effete – middle classes.

But what happens on the social and subjective level then? In 1848 Marx provided an amazing description of it, in that it is far truer today than it was in his own time. Let me quote an excerpt from this old text that has remained incredibly youthful:

> The bourgeoisie, wherever it has got the upper hand, has put an end to all feudal, patriarchal, idyllic relations. It has pitilessly torn asunder the motley feudal ties that bound man to his "natural superiors," and has left remaining no other nexus between man and man than naked self-interest, than callous "cash payment." It has drowned the most heavenly ecstasies of religious fervour, of chivalrous enthusiasm, of philistine sentimentalism, in the icy water of egotistical calculation. It has resolved personal worth into exchange value, and in place of the numberless indefeasible chartered freedoms, has set up that single, unconscionable freedom – Free Trade. In one word, for exploitation, veiled by religious and political illusions, it has substituted naked, shameless, direct, brutal exploitation.
>
> The bourgeoisie has stripped of its halo every occupation hitherto honoured and looked up to with reverent awe. It has converted the physician, the lawyer, the priest, the poet, the man of science, into its paid wage labourers.
>
> The bourgeoisie has torn away from the family its

sentimental veil, and has reduced the family relation
to a mere money relation.

[…] All fixed, fast-frozen relations, with their train
of ancient and venerable prejudices and opinions, are
swept away, all new-formed ones become antiquated
before they can ossify. All that is solid melts into air,
all that is holy is profaned, and man is at last com-
pelled to face with sober senses his real conditions of
life, and his relations with his kind.[5]

What Marx is describing here is how the abandonment of tradition has actually ushered in a
gigantic crisis in humanity's symbolic organization. Indeed, for millennia, the differences
inherent in human life were coded and symbolized in a hierarchical form. The most important
dichotomies, such as young and old, women and
men, poor and powerful, my group and other
groups, foreigners and nationals, heretics and
faithful, commoners and nobles, town and country, intellectuals and manual workers, were all
dealt with – in language, in the mythologies, in
the ideologies, in the established religious ethics
– by order structures, which defined everyone's

5 *Manifesto of the Communist Party*, https://www.marxists.
org/archive/marx/works/1848/communist-manifesto/ch01.htm.

place in overlapping hierarchical systems. Thus, a noblewoman was inferior to her husband but superior to a commoner; a rich bourgeois had to bow to a duke, but his servants had to bow to him. Similarly, a squaw from one Indian tribe or another was almost nothing in comparison with a warrior from her own tribe, but almost everything in comparison with a prisoner from another tribe, for whom she would often decide on the method of torture to be used. Or a poor Catholic believer was insignificant next to his bishop but could regard himself as one of the elect in comparison with a Protestant heretic, just as the son of a free man was wholly dependent on his father, but could have the black father of a huge family as his own personal slave.

The whole traditional symbolization was thus based on the order structure that assigned people's places, and therefore the relations between these places. The abandonment of tradition, as achieved by capitalism as a general system of production, trade, and ultimately places in society – these latter reduced to a dominant variant of the opposition between capital and labor, between profit and wages – did not actually propose any real symbolization but only the ruthless, arbitrary free play of the economy, the neutral, a-symbolic reign of what Marx so brilliantly called the "icy water of egotistical calculation." The abandonment of the hierarchically ordered world of tradition did not propose a non-hierarchical symbolization but only a violent real constraint under the yoke of the economy, accompanied by rules of calculation subject only to the appetites of a few. The result is a historic crisis of symbolization, in which young people today are suffering their disorientation.

When it comes to this crisis, which, under the pretext of a neutral freedom, proposes nothing but money as a universal referent, there are two distinct alternatives today – both of them absolutely reactionary, to my mind, and inadequate for the real subjective issues that humanity, and its youth in particular, are facing.

The first is the never-ending defense of capitalism and its empty "freedoms," undermined as they are by the sterile neutrality of market determination alone. Let's call this alternative the appeal to what I call "the desire for the West," or the assertion that there is, and can only be, nothing better than the liberal, "democratic" model of our society, here in France and in all the other countries of the same type. As Pascal Bruckner rather inanely entitled one of his articles a short time ago, "The Western way of life is not negotiable."[6]

The second alternative is the reactive desire for a return to traditional – that is, hierarchical – symbolization. This desire is often concealed in the guise of some religious narrative or other, whether it's a question of Protestant sects in the US, reactionary Islamism in the Middle East, or the return to ritualistic Judaism in Europe. But it can also lurk within nationalistic hierarchies (Long live the "native born" French! Long live Great Russian Orthodoxy!), pure and simple racism (Islamophobia of colonial origin, or recurrent anti-Semitism), or, ultimately, atomistic individualism (Up with Me, down with everyone else!).

In my view, both these alternatives are extremely dangerous dead-ends, and the increasingly bloody contradiction between them is pushing humanity into an endless cycle of wars. This is the whole problem of false contradictions, which prevent the free play of the true contradiction.

6 "Le mode de vie occidental n'est pas négociable," *Libération*, February 15, 2015.

This true contradiction, which ought to serve as our guide for both thought and action, pits two visions of the inevitable abandonment of the hierarchizing symbolic tradition against each other: Western capitalism's a-symbolic vision, which produces monstrous inequalities and pathogenic disorientation, and the vision commonly known as "communism," which, ever since the time of Marx and his contemporaries, has been proposing the creation of an egalitarian symbolization. After the provisional historical failure of state "communism" in the USSR and China, this fundamental contradiction of the modern world is now obscured by the false contradiction, with respect to the abandonment of tradition, between the West's neutral, sterile pure negativity, which destroys the old symbolic hierarchies in favor of real hierarchies concealed by monetary neutrality, and the fascistic reaction that advocates, with spectacular violence calculated to disguise its actual powerlessness, the return to the old hierarchies.

This contradiction is especially false in that, even though they brandish his dead body, the leaders and real beneficiaries of reactive fascism are by no means true believers in the dead God – the God who, in the old world, was both the pinnacle, the guarantee of, and the key to, the hierarchized symbolic order. They actually belong to the same world as the big Western finance groups: they both agree that no global organization of societies other than concentrated, predatory capitalism is possible. Neither offers humanity anything new in the way of symbolism. Where they disagree is only in how they evaluate the social capacity, the capacity for collective organization, the "icy water of egotistical calculation." As far as our Western overlords are concerned, that's all that's needed for humanity, with its super-rich elite and its enormous plebeian masses, to go on. Money will serve as an intangible symbol. As far as the reactionaries of all stripes are concerned, we need to return to the old morality and the divinely established hierarchies, or else, in the long run, there will be serious civil unrest that will jeopardize the overall system itself.

This dispute primarily serves both sides' interests, however bitter the conflict between them may seem. Thanks to their control of the media, the dispute captures the public's attention and thus prevents the advent of the only comprehensive conviction that can save humanity from disaster. This conviction – which I sometimes call "the communist Idea" – holds that, after the inevitable abandonment of tradition has been accepted, in the very process of this abandonment, we must work to create an egalitarian symbolization that will guide, code, and form the peaceful subjective basis for the collectivization of resources, the effective elimination of inequalities, the recognition of differences, with equal subjective rights, and, ultimately, the withering away of separate, state-type entities.

It is in the context of this need for an egalitarian symbolization that I can return to the subject of the young, who, along with the elderly, are the first to be affected by the reign of the false contradiction.

You young people are immersed in the dual effects of the real abandonment of tradition and the imaginary dimension of the false contradiction. You are at the same time, I believe, on the brink of a new world, the world of egalitarian symbolization. It's not an easy job: up until now, all the social symbolizations have been hierarchical ones. So you need to devote your subjective selves to a completely new task: creating a new symbolization opposed to the destruction of the symbolic in the icy water of capitalist calculation and to reactive fascism. That's why you also have a duty to be attentive (and this is the hardest part) to what's going on, to what's happening to young people – eternal adolescence, unemployment, differences based on one's origins and beliefs, the disorientation of life – but also to the new relationships, between the sexes, with adults, with the elderly, and with young people all over the world . . . There's all that, and there are also the signs of what might happen, of what might contribute to building a future able to be symbolized. These signs are often unclear and hidden, but philosophers have a duty to be attentive not just to what is going on but to what, in their own experience, strikes them as most unusual, unique, exceptional: as a sign pointing to what is to come rather than to what merely is.

There is nothing more important for everyone, but particularly for young people, than being attentive to the signs that something different from what is happening might happen. You'll find these signs if you observe attentively and discuss methodically everything that's going on in the wider world. But you can also find them in your life experiences, in what is exceptional and unique about them. To put it another way, there's what you're capable of – building your life, using what you're capable of – but there's also what you don't yet know you're capable of, which is actually the most important thing, the thing most related to the future egalitarian symbolization – namely, what you discover when you encounter something that was unforeseeable. For example, when you fall in love for good. You realize then that you're capable of things you didn't know you were capable of, that you had a hitherto unknown capacity, including in the order of thought, of symbol creation. This revelation that you're capable of much more than you thought you were can also occur when you take part in a movement for a new idea of collective life; when you feel the first stirrings of an artistic vocation because you've been deeply affected by a book, a piece of music, or a painting; or when you're drawn to some new scientific problems. In all these cases, you discover a capacity in yourself that you were unaware of.

We might say that there's what you can build, but there's also what makes you go away; there's what makes you settle down, but there's also your capacity for wandering, for taking off. There are both at once. Settling down can be countered by a kind of wandering that is no longer nihilistic but guided, a compass to help you find the true life, a new symbol.

This last point, which is related to the opposition I began with between burning up one's life and building it, is something that, whether consciously or unconsciously, constitutes young people's subjectivity. I would say that a connection needs to be made between the two. There is what you want to build, what you're capable of, but there are also the signs of what compels you to leave, to go beyond what you're able to do, build, or settle into. The power of departure. Building and leaving. There's no contradiction between them. Being able to give up what you're building because something else has beckoned you toward the true life. The true life, today, beyond market neutrality and beyond the old, outdated hierarchical ideas.

As regards all this, I'll let the poet have the last words, because, when it comes to this question of departure, displacement, self-uprooting, and newly invented symbols, the poets are adept at finding a new language. Poetry, in this sense, is the fixing of an eternal youth in language. I'm going to use a passage from the end of a poem by Saint-John Perse, a poet of the 1920s–50s, and this poem is called "Anabasis." The word *anabasis* in Greek means "to return by going back up." It's a wandering that returns, or goes back up, to a hard-to-reach destination. That's why it is a metaphor for youth.

Anabasis is the title of a Greek book that tells the story of mercenaries fighting in a civil war in Persia. The book's author is Xenophon, who was one of the officers of the mercenaries. There were already mercenaries back then, just as there are today in all the wars in Africa or the Middle East, or even in central Europe. They are people who are not really concerned about what happens on the political level. They do their brutal job as soldiers in the pay of an employer. In the case of Xenophon's book, the Persian employer is killed in a big battle, all the other Persian soldiers disband, the Greek mercenaries are left in the middle of Persia – today's Turkey – and, with unwavering determination, they resolve to return home, to head North. They're completely stranded and have to head homeward. That's the idea. You are abandoned, disoriented, and yet you think you can head toward what you're capable of being, toward what your authentic reality is. The subject that you are can never be realized just by building its house solidly. It also needs to move toward itself. The old house is merely tradition, and the wandering you undergo gives it a new affirmation. You then have a new symbolization of your own site. A true house is something you can return to when the adventure of thought and action has made you leave it and almost forget about it. A house you stay in forever is just a voluntary prison. When something important happens in life it is always like a departure, an uprooting, directed toward whatever the true life is for you. Anabasis is the idea that you're disoriented but that you'll move toward yourself, find your true self within this disorientation and this departure, and, together with all humanity, create the stages of an egalitarian symbolization.

There is a wonderful scene in Xenophon's *Anabasis*. The mercenaries are Greeks, hence sailors. As they go back up north, they come upon the sea again. They've gone back up and they've also climbed up: they're there, at the top of a hill, and they see the sea. And they all cry out "*Thalassa! Thalassa!*", "The sea! The sea!" They re-symbolize their old sailor selves affirmatively.

46

Youth is this sort of thing, too; it has to be: an anabasis toward the ocean of the world.

Nowadays, because they have freedom and opportunity, the young are no longer bound by tradition. But what should be done with this freedom, with this new chance to wander? You need to find out what you're capable of as regards a creative, intense true life. You need to return to your own capacity. It is there that you'll be ready for the new egalitarian symbolization. That is the relationship between construction and its opposite. Its metaphor, for the Greek mercenaries, is the suddenly discovered relationship between farmer, soldier, and sailor. It's the cry that expresses what they lost in the earthly adventure of life and found again, not in terms of a mere return or repetition but in terms of its intense, new meaning: "*Thalassa*! The sea!" The sea transformed into a symbol not of the old condition but of the new egalitarian sharing of an incredible experience.

Here, along these same lines, is the conclusion of Saint-John Perse's poem "Anabasis":

but over and above the actions of men on the earth, many omens on the way, many seeds on the way, and under unleavened fine weather, in one great breath of the earth, the whole feather of harvest! . . .

until the hour of evening when the female star, pure and pledged in the sky heights . . .

Plough-land of dream! Who talks of building? – I have seen the earth parcelled out in vast spaces and my thought is not heedless of the navigator.[7]

So, is being young today an advantage or a drawback? The world will have to change if it is to welcome its new youth into a world relentlessly free of traditions. The new earth will also be the "plough-land of dream" of all the young people who will create – who are already creating – the new thinking, the new systems of symbolization that the new world needs. Building is no doubt necessary; founding is necessary. But the world is vast, and it is on its scale that thinking must perceive and act. I can only hope, for all of you, that settling down, having a job, a career, is not your top priority, but rather a true thinking that is sister to the dream. A thinking of departure, a true thinking of the ever-changing ocean of the

7 "Anabasis," tr. T. S. Eliot in *Selected Poems of Saint-John Perse*, ed. Mary Ann Caws (New York: New Directions, 1982), 43.

world. An exact and nomadic thinking, an exact thinking because it is a nomadic one, a maritime thinking. May everyone be able to say: "I have seen the earth parcelled out in vast spaces and my thought is not heedless of the navigator."

2

About the contemporary fate of boys

Plato considered the question "What can the philosopher say to young people?" to be the most important philosophical question by far.

In the previous chapter, I already answered this question to a large extent but without bringing the (in fact, crucial) subject of sexual difference into it. In this chapter, I am going to speak about the fate of boys. All that will be left for me to do is speak about girls, and I'll do that in the third and final chapter.

I dedicate what I'll be saying here to my three sons, Simon, André, and Olivier. They have all taught me, in a pretty tough way at times, what a son is, for both himself and his parents.

I'd like to begin with a conceptual myth: the

unit formed by *Totem and Taboo* and *Moses and Monotheism* in Freud's work. In the style of founding figures, *à la* Hegel, Freud tells us a story in three lengthy chapters. First, there's the chapter on the primal horde, in which the pleasure-seeking father monopolizes all the women, and the sons' revolt paves the way for the father's murder. This is the origin of a pact by which the sons organize themselves to handle the situation in as egalitarian a way as possible. The second chapter deals with the sublimation of the dead father into the Law in the figure of the one God. The father is once again a strict guardian and a stern protector, but it is important to understand that the murdered *real* father only returns in the guise of the *symbolic* father. The third chapter deals with the son's participation in the father's glory, in Christianity, at the price of a very violent initiation: the son of God's initiation into what humanity imposes on itself in the way of torture and death.

I have three comments to make about what we can learn from this story today, insofar as the structure within it speaks for itself, as it were.

First, concerning the father. In the first episode, we meet a real father, a father of *jouissance*, a father who refuses to give up his monopoly on *jouissance*. And we see that, where the son is concerned, the operative, no less real, factor is an aggression that can only be satisfied by murder. In the second episode, we've got the symbolic father, who is based on the real father but who returns in the guise of the Other, as Lacan would say. In terms of the son, we find, as though by a reversal of the aggression aroused by the real father, devotion to the big Other, and therefore a figure of boundless submission. In the third episode, that of Christianity, one would be tempted to say we've got the imaginary father. Indeed, the father is relegated to the back of the stage, as it were; he is like the backdrop for the son's action. He becomes the imaginary totality of the three orders: he is the father, and the trinity as well. But in both the real and the symbolic these three orders are untotalizable, so the father can only be akin to semblance.

These are the basic figures of the father in Freud's account.

But it's the son we're concerned with here. In this myth, the son's becoming is a dialectical construction – indeed, the model for all classical dialectical constructions. Because, while the

son eventually reaches a place where full reconciliation with the father is achieved – the son
consubstantial with the father, the son who sits at
the right hand of the father, etc. – he only does
so after completing three stages: the immediate,
violent stage of aggression; the symbolic stage
of submission to the law; and the final stage of
mutual love. Love as the sublation of the murder
through the mediation of the Law: such is the
son's destiny. Concrete revolt, abstract submission, mutual love.

It is very important to note the role of initiation in this dialectical becoming. The son can
only be introduced into the ultimate order of
reconciliation by undergoing an initiation that
marks the body, an initiation into torture and
death, whose extraordinary iconographic destiny
is well known. The son's crucified body is the
radical figure of the infinite God's initiation into
terrifying finitude. Thus, when the son returns to
the bosom of the father through the aptly named
process of "Ascension," a sign of the original violence, traced on the body of the resurrected man,
is preserved.

This is a coherent construct, one that is very
satisfying to the optimistic philosopher, even if

he or she is an atheist, because it preserves the notion of stages and yet results in a reconciled figure of humanity's fate.

The problem is that, today, this construct is being undermined on both its sides. On the side of the father, because he can only be thought with difficulty now, as both real and symbolic, at least insofar as he is seen by the son. Indeed, what I'm concerned about today is the father as seen by the son. So I can say that, as the father of *jouissance* and as the father of the Law, he is a problematic figure. As far as *jouissance* is concerned, it is the father nowadays who tends to envy the son's *jouissance*. There is, in fact, the modern phenomenon of the cult of youth, of the young body, not just as an object but also, and above all, as a subject. The father has long been depicted as an old, and maybe even lecherous, man. It is clear that that figure, given everything that contemporary society provides in the way of *jouissance*, has become almost invisible now. By the way, I would say that one of the characteristics of our society is to make old age as invisible as possible. Little by little, the real father is being relegated to this social invisibility. By the same token, as the symbolic father, he is also in the difficult position of having to endure the son's gaze, since the most evident law is now external to him. This law is that of the market, which is characterized by equating everything with everything else, by being an anonymous law, with the result that the figure of the father has been cut off from it, and any control of the sons is itself a-symbolic. It is unable to serve as the law of the father, to whom justice is to be done. Anarchic, at once non-existent and excessive, the social control of the sons becomes detached from the power of the symbol.

Should we say that the father tends to be only imaginary now? That would be the triumph of what might be called a Christianity without God. Christianity, because the son has been elevated to the status of the new hero of the story, which, in commodified modernity, amounts to nothing but fashion, consumption, and representation, all native attributes of youth. But without God, which means without any true symbolic order, because, even though the sons rule, they only do so over semblance now.

In sum, already as regards the father, the considerable difficulty of establishing a stable identity for the son can be seen. Indeed, the son's identity is shaky because his dialectic has broken down. And this dialectic breaks down not because its constitutive figures disappear but because they gradually become separated or detached.

Let's analyze things descriptively. One of the sons' fundamental structures, particularly among working-class youth, is the gang, the famous, much-feared "youth gang." In a way, it reproduces what Freud called "the horde," and that's why it is considered a scourge of society. The problem is clearly that it's a fatherless horde, which therefore has no possibility of committing a salvific murder and forging a genuine pact between the brothers. Rather than deriving from a pact made between its members in the act by which their aggression is turned against the father, its consistency derives from a mimetic separation. The gang is separate; it has its own rules. But this separation is also a sameness and a similarity, because its purpose is the circulation of commodities, in the figure of endless trading, buying, and ultimately trafficking. It is territorialized, but this territorialization is symmetrical: the territory is only ever the mirror-image of another, disputed territory. The gang creates nothing but a sort of stationary nomadism. Aggression, the time when the horde develops, is uninterrupted here. It is unable to focus itself in a foundational act. But non-foundational aggression is doomed to repetition, and therefore ultimately governed by the death drive.

So much for the first stage of the sons' dialectic, the stage in which aggression develops.

What about the second stage, the one in which submission to the law arises? There is, of course, a relationship to the law in gangs, but it is split between, on the one hand, an imperative of representation regarding customs, dress, language, gestures, and so on, which once again dissolves the law in the mimetics of semblance, and, on the other hand, an imperative of inertia, which dictates simple self-perpetuation rather than transformative action. The point is to keep going on, in a state of permanent passivity. The imperative of action that led to the sons' pact becomes commodity circulation; the imperative that was the law becomes the production of inertia.

The third stage of the son's dialectic is the one in which initiation comes into play. This initiation, from being outside the law, as it were, has become immanent. It is no longer something that makes the passage to another figure possible. On the contrary, it is a rite of incorporation into the sons' stasis. It is all the stereotypical practices that lead to the collective acceptance of inertia. This initiation, unlike the kind that establishes you as an adult, fosters the myth of an eternal adolescence.

As a result, the reconciliation of the son and the adult, of sons and parents, of the son and the father, can only be achieved through the infantilization of the adult. It is seemingly feasible, except that it is inverted. In primitive Christian mythology, there was the son's ascension. Now, all that's offered are empirical processes of the decline of fathers.

For all these reasons, the dialectical schema in Freud's myth has collapsed, with the result that there is no clear proposition concerning the son's identity. This is what could be called the uncertainty of the son's identity in the world today.

There is a rationality to this uncertainty. It's not some awful, inexplicable catastrophe. It is part of the rational development of our society. It is the consequence of a progressively universal conditioning of the individual to be someone who faces the glittering marketplace. The most important societal imperative is to ensure that all real individuality is dependent on the circulation of commodities. So, if there is a subjectivation of this individuality, it must be the kind that makes the individual want to face the vast array of commodities on offer and have the ability, however great or small, to make them circulate. For this very reason, the individual is gradually prevented from becoming the subject he or she is capable of being. As we know, boys are central to all this, because adolescence is the heart of the market. Adolescence is the time of fundamental conditioning in the service of market competition, the time of initiation into the market itself. A becoming-subject wholly subservient to the circulation of commodities and the sterile communication of signs and images is imposed on individuals who are vulnerable and conformist, as everyone is at that age.

So I think – this is a hypothesis – that this initiation without initiation offers boys three alternatives. I'll call them: the perverted body, the sacrificed body, and the deserving body.

First, the perverted body. This means taking onto one's body itself the mark of the end of the old dialectic. So a long, pointless, a-symbolic initiation has to be undergone, which inscribes the abandonment of the dialectic on bodies.

Piercing the body, drugging it, deadening it with ear-splitting music, tattooing it. This is the figure of a body that one wants to make a-subjective, or even a-subjectivizable, a body exposed and marked, which preserves within itself the trace of the impossible identity. This bears a superficial resemblance to the initiations practiced in some traditional societies. But there is a radical change in its role, because it is an initiation not into childbearing for women or war for men but into the inertia of eternal adolescence. The sexuality to which this type of choice leads I would call, descriptively, "pornographic," with no particular value judgment. What I mean by "pornographic" is an a-subjective sexuality. It is based on the marking of the body in the repetition of inertia. Gang rape can certainly be a figure of this pornography, as can undeniable sexual deprivation, forced abstinence, in the face of the deluge of images. In any case, there is an absence of any ideas. What we have is the depressing construction of a body without ideas. This is the body I call "perverted" – without any allusion to the so-called "perversions" – but "perverted" in the sense that it has been diverted from its normal purpose, which is to be the repository for a subject.

At the other extreme, there is the sacrificed body. This is a body trying desperately to bring tradition back. The old, deathly law is turned to as something to which the new body can and must submit. The perverted body must be kept at bay, including through the use of purification rituals – entailing extreme sexual puritanism – and the absoluteness of the law must be accepted, to the point of self-sacrifice. This is the subjective figure of the young man as a terrorist. The body's motivation is driven by loathing of the perverted body, which must be offered up as the filial sacrifice to the Father's absoluteness under the conditions of an inexorable return to the old law, the most immutable law conceivable. The body's subjectivation is that of its martyrdom.

These are two extreme but real positions. Between them, there is the acceptance of everyday conditioning, making oneself into a fit commodity for international trade, which can also be called "pursuing a career," or, in Sarkozy's terms, "being deserving." This time, the body will place itself in a position calculated to be best suited to the external laws of the market. It will itself become part of the organized circulation that will be held to be the only acceptable law, that of "the general equivalent," as Marx called it a long time ago. The deserving body positions itself on the market at the best price. To do so, it has to be protected, defended, against the combined threats of the other two bodies, a task essentially undertaken by the police.

Just as an aside, as regards what happened in France, in Clichy in Fall 2005, and in Greece in 2008, it was of course "sons and daughters of the working class," as they used to say back in the days of the communist parties, who were in the spotlight. I'd just like to point out that it is wrong to view this problem as an essentially social one, if what is meant by that is something having to do with the economy – or, even worse, if it's assumed that the problem would be fixed by throwing more money at the so-called *banlieues* or the universities. It is a problem symptomatic of contemporary society, a problem that might be called a political symptom. The problem is a question of what happens to boys when they're excluded from the everyday conditioning, from the fast – but meaningless – track reserved for the deserving body. Everyone knows that the non-deserving body is treated like the enemy of the deserving body, from which it must be segregated at all costs, thus creating the problems of educational and professional apartheid as well as the critical problem of the police, who are used to keep the different bodies apart.

It is undeniable that the police have a particular relationship with the young people – who are overwhelmingly from the working classes, from the working people, and whose parents are often of foreign origin – the young people who neither can nor want to identify as deserving bodies. These young people say – and this is the main reason for their rebellion – "The police are always on our backs." This unfortunately comes with the territory, given that the deserving body's protected status requires fiercely guarded walls. A couple of deaths here, a couple of deaths there, constant arrests, young people jailed *en masse*: isn't it right, then, to rebel against the police, and the state that supports them, including by lying? Well, it's the rebels who get attacked in the press and in politicians' speeches, not the police or the state. The propaganda claims that these regrettable deaths are the price that must be paid if we want young men who are obedient, not through submission to the father but through submission to money and its "free circulation," the real content of this fetishized democracy that takes the place of Ideas for us when there are none left.

Let me return to my subject now: the three types of bodies constitute the space of what I would call the dis-initiated son, the son to whom no initiation is offered, in the sense of transmission, passing of the torch, the future. This space is thoroughly nihilistic, even though the purpose of the deserving body is to conceal the nihilism: to make it seem as though having a career actually meant something. The career is the hole-plugger of meaninglessness. That's the role of docile youth. It is important to understand that it's this motley herd that will sooner or later be led to the abyss of war to confirm its meaninglessness once and for all. I don't know what kind of war it will be, but the uncertainty of the sons' identity does not promise peace, let alone that the total vacuity of deserving bodies will be idolized.

The issue of war is very important here. In modern times, the times ushered in by the French Revolution, the state's part in the sons' initiation was symbolized by the figure of the soldier. That has become completely foreign to us for some years now. But it was a major factor for 200 years. Military service: that was the initiatic break. It brought the boys together and, in so doing, made a radical distinction between them and the girls. This was a first, necessary stage of identity. Second, it gave shape and discipline to aggression. It recognized its usefulness; it did not simply suppress aggression but disciplined it and constructed a right to violence. Finally, it reconciled the officer-father and the soldier-son under a symbol: they both saluted the flag, that colorful embodiment of transcendence. Military service was part of the dialectical configuration I began with: the disciplined preservation of aggression carried to the extreme of the right to murder; repressive symbolism and complete submission; reconciliation, at least on the surface, in the form of "sons of the homeland." As an institution – like every institution, horrible and stupid, but functional – military service provided a laicization of archaic filiation rites. The son was subject to military service, after which came an occupation and a family, and then he was an adult.

The consequences of the abolition of compulsory military service have not been faced well. Abolishing it was probably inevitable, in an imperialistic France shorn of its military glory, reduced to the rank of a middling power, and anxious not to spend too much. Along the same lines, symbolic equality was no longer defined by patriotic death and its emblems but only by the triviality of money. And, in fact, not a single bourgeois can still imagine having to die, as an officer, for France. This is why there is, symbolically, no ruling class anymore. There is just an irresponsible oligarchy. So the army, contrary to Jaurès's hopes before World War I (he was against a professional army and for an army composed exclusively of citizen soldiers, organized exclusively for defense), is just a bunch of mercenaries now. Let me pay tribute one last time to military service and all it stood for, even in the ignominy of war, with respect to the very complex question of the sons' fate.

Does this mean that State initiation is over? They're trying to make us believe that school has become the peaceful institution of public initiation. I'm highly skeptical about that. Public education is in no better shape than military service was in its final years of existence. Widely acknowledged as being of key importance, the crisis in education is only just beginning. The processes of dismantlement, privatization, social segregation, and educational inadequacy are going to accelerate. Why? Because we no longer require schools to deliver shared knowledge or even proper worker training to the broad masses. We require them – and this will increasingly be their role – to separate out and protect the deserving bodies. I don't think school can take over from the military. I even think that school, which is always selective and dedicated to "merit," has implicitly assumed that the military was where real equality was achieved, in facing the risk of death. As for its symbolic functions of initiation, the contemporary "democratic" state is bankrupt.

Perhaps today's sons, with their unstable identities, are the symptom of some deep-rooted disease afflicting the state. It is perhaps in our sons that we can see the outcome of that old, long-since abandoned prediction of Marx's, the withering away of the state. Marx, under the banner of communism, gave us its revolutionary version, which restored the whole dialectic of the sons in the context of equality and comprehensive universal knowledge. Is what we have today the reactive, watered-down version of withering away? The "democratic" state's capacity for symbolization has at any rate been seriously undermined. Perhaps it's through our sons that we are faced more than ever with the strategic choice between two opposite forms of the withering away of the state: communism or barbarism.

So how can the new symbolic situation be envisioned positively, beyond the symptom of the sons? How will we avoid an apocalyptic outcome of the problem, that of a total and totally a-symbolic war?

We'll be guided, as we always are in moments of confusion in thought and life, by what remains in terms of new truths, or, in my terminology, of generic procedures made possible by some event.

For example, what can certainly keep the perverted body, or the body without ideas, at bay is love – reinvented perhaps, as Rimbaud put it. Because love, the experience in living thought of the Two, alone can free the son's body from the pornographic solitude of the perverted body.

To put an end to the sacrificed body, we need to turn to political life, a political life that would be capable of providing a strong, effective figure of disinterested discipline to counter the law of commodified representation and suicidal adolescent inertia. A politics that must turn away from power, since the state no longer has the symbolic means to assume responsibility for the sons' initiation. To combat the influence of religion, which is just a desperate substitute, a return to obsolete symbols, we'll propose, in organized collective action, a non-deadening discipline, which finds its founding thought within itself. We'll pit the enthusiasm of all the militants together, the improbable gathering of subjects from far and wide, against both the disaffected gang and the futile, mournful martyr.

The subject's recourse against the deserving body, which uses knowledge or proficiency to get ahead career-wise, lies in the disinterestedness of true intellectual creativity, the disinterested joys of science and art, the idea's insubordination to the money-oriented world of technology.

Under these conditions, which he is both a symptom of and a contributor to, the son will become able to move a step closer to the father that he will one day be. A father unlike any fathers who came before.

I think that Rimbaud, whom we definitely need to re-read, had already seen something of this triad of love, politics, and art–science, in which the fate of a different kind of filiation is at stake. A filiation that would not be a return to the old law and would thereby do away with the sacrificed body.

Rimbaud anticipated the perverted body; he experimented with it and called it the "derangement of all the senses." He experimented with the sacrificed body, which he called "the race" or "Christ," when he wrote [in *A Season in Hell*]: "I am of the race that sang under torture" ("Bad Blood," 17). And then he reconciled himself to the deserving body. He gave up dreams and poetry and became a trader, an arms dealer, and sent money back home to his mother: "I who called myself angel or seer, exempt from all morality, I am returned to the soil with a duty to seek and rough reality to embrace" ("Adieu," 87). Rimbaud's meteoric life is a lightning-quick survey of the modern history of the son. It was he who said, in modern terms and with a new meaning, "Father, Father, why hast thou forsaken me?" As we know, in the Gospel this is said at the time when, on the eve of Christ's crucifixion, death, and finally Ascension, there is the ordeal of abandonment. And this hopeless abandonment is the cross that the sons bear today.

Yet, in spite of having ultimately opted for business, Rimbaud knew that a different vision of the son was possible, a different initiation, a different subjectivizable body, which escapes a different triad – a bodily one – of perversion, martyrdom, and conformism. He spoke about this in the poem "Genie." This poem, among other things, describes the joy aroused in Rimbaud's mind by the fleeting impression of a redemption or a possible salvation of the new figure of the son's body. He wrote: "His body! The dreamed-of release, the shattering of grace crossed with new violence!"[1] That could be the guiding principle of our work together in the service of the new initiation of the sons.

I never stop repeating: the philosopher's role has always been to corrupt youth. This role takes on a very special meaning today: to help ensure that the question of the sons, no longer subject to the typology of the three bodies, is restored to truths. The philosopher cannot resign himself to the lesser evil that the deserving body represents in the eyes of so many fathers and mothers. Yes, in love, science, and politics, there may be a kind of grace – or, in other words, something,

1 *Illuminations*, tr. Louise Varese (New York: New Directions, 1957), 137.

71

concerning the body, that gives it back the missing idea. There may be a shattering that this grace produces in the individual who, in thrall to commodities and Capital, is separated from the subject he is capable of being. That subject is given back to him by the shattering. And there will also be, not the reactive myth of "human rights" and the end of all violence, which is only ever the reign of police violence and endless wars, but the "new violence," through which the sons will affirm, for the joy of real fathers, the new world they aim to create.

No, we won't resign ourselves to the submissive blandness of the deserving body, just because of perverted bodies and sacrificed bodies surrounded by barbaric police. It is not true that the sons' bodies are doomed to what Lacan called "the service of goods," a service that keeps subjects from doing their duty – that is, from coming into being as Subjects. As the local work of truths that philosophy universalizes goes on, there will be grace, shattering, and the new violence.

Long live our sons and daughters!

3

About the contemporary fate of girls

I am hesitant as I approach this issue.

First of all, speaking about girls, young girls, or young women, when you're a man getting on in years, is very dangerous in itself. May my only daughter, Claude Ariane, encourage me in pursuing this perilous path. Second of all, it is by no means certain that there is a "girl question" in the contemporary world. In the old world, the world of tradition, the girl question was easy: it had to do with whether and how a girl was going to get married, how she was going to switch from the status of attractive virgin to that of overburdened mother. Between the two, moreover, between the girl and the mother, there was that negative and despised figure, the unwed mother [*la fille-mère*, literally, "the girl-mother"], who was no longer a girl, since she was a mother, and wasn't really a mother, since she was unwed and therefore still a girl.

The figure of the unwed mother was fundamental in traditional society, as it was in all nineteenth-century fiction. It already showed that, when faced with any conceptual duality, any duality of places, a woman can construct an in-between place, a place outside of place, neither girl nor mother, for example. She can thus be what Georges Bataille called "the accursed share" [*la part maudite*]. In traditional society, the accursed share is always a woman's share. The unwed mother is one such instance. The old maid is another. By definition, a girl must be young. And so an old maid is another place that is not a place. The theme of the out-of-place place is an absolutely classical structural theme. It will nevertheless serve as a guiding thread for me, at my own peril.

In the contemporary world – the world of unbridled capitalism, commodities, salaried employment, circulation, and communication – the girl's position can no longer be completely reduced to the logic of marriage. Of course, the old world is far from being completely dead. Religion, family, marriage, motherhood, modesty, even virginity itself, are still on a solid footing in many places around the world. But what the philosopher cares about is less what *is* than what is to come. And what is to come, as regards girls, can no longer be completely reduced to marriage. A girl in the contemporary Western world cannot be defined as a person of the female sex who prepares for her becoming-woman-and-mother through the mediation of marriage, and therefore through the mediation of a man. Ultimately, the whole feminist movement, since the late nineteenth century, comes down to just one issue: a woman can and must exist without being dependent on a man. A woman can and must be an autonomous person and not always the product of male mediation. Despite significant ambiguities that I'll come back to, this movement has led to important changes, which particularly affect the status, and even the definition, of a girl.

In the world of tradition, male mediation constituted the girl question in the following sense: what separated the girl from the woman was the man. It was completely different for boys, because what separated the son from the father was not a real external term, as was a husband. What separated the son from the father was control over the symbolic order. The son had to take over from the father; he had to take power in his turn. He had to become the master of the Law. You could say that, between the girl and the woman-mother, there was the man, an instance of real pure exteriority, to whom she surrendered her body; to whom, as people used to say, she "gave herself"; to whom she belonged. Whereas between the son and the man-father, there was the Law.

The girl of the traditional world gave up her own name for the man's; she became "Mrs. X." She could thus remain apart from salaried employment, run the household, be first and foremost a mother, and, more specifically, a *mère de famille*, a "mother of a family." In the reactionary triad "Work, Family, Homeland," the worker and the farmer, symbolically male categories, were dedicated to work; the soldier, no less a male category, was dedicated to the homeland; and the girl who had become a mother symbolized the family. The triad contained two male categories, work and homeland, as against only one female one, the family.

In the traditional world, this "two-to-one" phenomenon afflicting women was very common. Consider the French marriage law, still in effect in the early 1960s, 50 years ago – which is nothing, in terms of history. The law stipulated that the husband had the right to choose the family home and that the wife had to live in that home. But it wasn't stipulated that the husband had to live there. So he had the right to lock his wife away in the house and also the right not to be there himself. Whereas the woman only had the duty to be in the house. Two to one in the man's favor: that is really the law of the traditional family.

But what is the family? Already in Plato there were three major social functions: producing, reproducing, and defending. Work was what produced, the family was the place of reproduction, and the homeland was what was defended. Between production and defense, the girl who had become a woman, confined to the labor of motherhood, ensured reproduction. Two to one, as usual. The traditional woman was the place in between the worker and the soldier. She welcomed to her table and into her bed the mature man who worked and was her husband. She patriotically mourned the young man fallen in combat who was her son. The girl had to become Mater Dolorosa. Two to one, again: the living father who controlled his wife's body and the dead son who controlled her tears.

Now, however, the traditional family is slowly but surely dying out, in our society. In the world to come, the contemporary world that's developing, a girl can choose to be a worker, a farmer, a teacher, an engineer, a police officer, a check-out employee, a soldier, or president of the Republic. She can live with a man outside marriage, have one lover, several lovers, or no lovers at all. She can get married then divorced, change where she lives or who she loves. She can live alone without being that other important, pitiful traditional figure, the old maid. She can have children without a husband, or even have children with another woman. She can get an abortion. The ugly label "unwed mother" is disappearing. For a time, people said "single mother" [*mère célibataire*], but that has already been superseded by something even more neutral, "the single-parent family" [*la famille monoparentale*]. And now a single-parent family can even be made up of a father and his children, with no woman at all.

And no one will speak of an "unwed father" the way they used to speak of an "unwed mother." The negative figure of the old maid itself can become the positive figure of the independent woman.

Yes, yes, I know: there is strong resistance to all this, it's not yet a done deal in many places, and even in our democratic European countries it's not accepted everywhere. But this is what is happening, this is what is coming. It is here that our question – our so-called question, the girl question – arises. Its first formulation might be: if the girl, or the young woman, is not separated from the woman by the real function of a man and the symbolic function of marriage, whatever can the principle of her existence be? And is she disoriented, as I said earlier in this book that boys were?

My theory about boys was as follows: the end of initiation rites, chief among them being military service, means that boys have no symbolic point of support to help them become different from what they are. The Idea is lacking too much for life to be something more than just its day-to-day continuation. Hence, the temptation of an eternal adolescence. Hence, too, what we see every day: the childishness of adults' lives, of male adults' lives in particular. The male subject who confronts commodities has to remain a child who wants new toys. As for the male subject who confronts the social and electoral order, he has to remain an obedient, unimaginative schoolchild whose only ambition is to be at the top of the class no matter what, and for his name to be on everyone's lips.

But what about girls? It could be argued that girls, too, are doomed to a lack of separation, between the being-girl and the being-woman, since men and marriage no longer play the role, both real and symbolic, of separation. My hypothesis is different, however. Here's what it is. With boys, the end of traditional initiation leads to a childlike stasis, which can be called a life without Ideas. With girls, the lack of external separation (men and marriage) between girl and woman, between young-woman and woman-mother, leads to the immanent construction of a womanhood that could be called premature. Or: boys are at risk of never becoming the adult they contain within themselves, while girls are at risk of having always already become the woman-adult that they ought to actively become. Or again: with boys, there is no anticipation, hence the anxiety of stasis. With girls, the retroaction of the adult on them consumes their adolescence, or even their childhood itself. Hence the anxiety of prematurity.

Look at most girls in modern society. They are no different from women; they are very young women, that's all. They dress and are made up like women, they speak like women, they know about everything. In the women's magazines that cater to these very young women, the topics are exactly the same as in all the other magazines: clothes, body care, shopping, hairstyles, what you need to know about men, astrology, jobs, and sex.

Under these conditions, what results is a sort of girl-woman prematurely constituted as an adult, with no need of anyone. This is the cause of the total decline of the symbol of virginity. The symbol of virginity is fundamental in traditional societies: it designates the proof in a girl's body that she has not yet encountered the sexual mediation of a man and that she is therefore not yet a woman. A girl is a virgin: that's symbolically all-important. But in contemporary society this symbol has been eliminated. Why? Because, even if she's empirically a virgin, a girl today is already a woman. She bears in herself the retroactive action of the woman that she will only become because she already *is* that woman, without the man's having anything much to do with it. We could also say that the poetic figure of the girl, which informs so many wonderful English novels, is irrelevant now: contemporary magazines for girls, which teach them how to pleasure men without running any risk and how to dress to turn them on, have wiped out poetry of that sort. The magazines are not at fault: all they do is address in every girl the contemporary woman she has already become and whose cynicism is, so to speak, innocent.

That's why girls are able to do with impeccable talent anything they're asked to do as children or as adolescents, given that they are now, all on their own, far superior to all that. If boys are forever immature, girls, on the contrary, have always been mature. Let me give just one example: academic success. A real gulf, in girls' favor, has opened up, especially in working-class communities. While school has been an unmitigated disaster for young males from the *banlieues*, their sisters are not just succeeding but are doing better than girls from affluent neighborhoods, who are themselves head and shoulders above the stupid rich boys. I myself have often seen poor young men of Arab origin, hauled from their working-class neighborhoods before the courts by the police, and the female lawyer, or even the judge, might have been their sister. Or else, given their sexual misery, these boys may have caught an STD, and the doctor treating them could easily be their sister or their female cousin. Wherever social and symbolic success is involved, the girl-woman will now triumph over the boy who is unable to get beyond his adolescence.

Which, by the way, shows that social deprivation is by no means the problem. The girls are just as badly off as the boys in the poor neighborhoods, or even worse off, because they often have to manage the household and take care of the younger kids. Working on a corner of the kitchen table, they are jubilant, knowing that the homework expected of them is mere child's play for them, definitive women as they are.

You could say it's because they want to escape the oppressive world they were born into. Well, of course! But the whole point is that they *can*. And it's only because the free woman they want to become is already within them in all her force, as fierce and self-assured as need be. While the boy, not knowing what he is, is unable to become what he can, the girl-woman can easily become what she already knows she is.

As a result, the girl question, as opposed to the boy question, no longer exists as such; only the woman question does. This woman that girls are prematurely, who is she? What is the figure of her?

Turning to contemporary figures of femininity now, I'd like to show what the real gendered mechanism of modern capitalist oppression is. It is no longer a matter, as in the world of tradition, of a direct subordination, at once real and symbolic – husband and marriage – of the woman-mother to the man-father. Instead, it's about promoting the imperative "Live without Ideas" everywhere. But the ways in which this imperative operates differ depending on whether it's boys or girls who are being made to submit to it. That life can be life without Ideas, or the stupid life – the subjectivity required by globalized capitalism – is obtained from young males by the impossibility of the becoming-adult, the eternal consumerist and competitive adolescence.

It is obtained from young females, on the other hand, by the impossibility for them of remaining girls, of basking in the glory of being a girl, and by a premature becoming-woman driven by the cynicism of social becoming.

What does contemporary society, in the clutches of the capitalist monster, want? It wants two things: for us to buy the products on the market if we can, and, if we can't, for us to just keep quiet. For both these things we need to have no idea of justice, no idea of a different future, no free thought. But all true thought is free. And since, in our world, the only thing that matters is something that has a price, we need to have no thoughts, no ideas. Only then can we obey the world that tells us: "Consume if you can afford to; otherwise shut up and get lost." Only then will we have a totally disoriented and repetitive life, since the compass that Ideas provide will have disappeared.

Traditional society is completely different, because it imposes a belief, and therefore an Idea. What's oppressive about it is not that you have to live without Ideas but that there's one obligatory, usually religious, Idea. Its imperative is "Live with *this* Idea and no other," whereas the contemporary imperative, let me repeat, is: "Live without *any* Ideas." That's why people have been talking about the death of ideologies for the past 40 years.

Basically, the traditional imperative is "Be a man just like your father, a woman just like your mother, and never change Ideas," whereas the contemporary imperative is instead: "Be the human animal that you are, full of little desires and without any Ideas whatsoever." But the ways of conditioning the individual animal differ – at any rate, now – depending on whether you're of the female sex, a girl, or of the male sex, a boy.

We could say that the boy will live without any Ideas because he wasn't able to undergo the maturing of a thought, while the girl will live without any Ideas because she has undergone far too soon and without any mediation a maturing process as fruitless as it is ambitious. The boy fails to have any Ideas through lack of Man, the girl, through excess of Woman.

Let's exaggerate things a bit. What might the world become under these conditions? It might become a herd of stupid adolescent boys led by smart career women. We'd then have something perfectly suited to the opaque and violent world being offered us: in terms of Ideas, there would only be things.

But let's get back to the figures of femininity as they have prematurely emerged in the place where the girl has disappeared. The circle of the figures of femininity, as constructed for thousands of years by male-dominated society, has four poles.

First, there's the woman as productive and reproductive domestic animal. The woman is thus considered to be situated between symbolic humanity governed by the Name-of-the-Father and pre-symbolic animality. This figure naturally includes motherhood, and it is the material basis of the other three figures. Second, there's the woman as seductress, the sexual, dangerous woman. Third, the woman as symbol of love, the woman of self-giving and passionate self-sacrifice. And last but not least, the woman as holy virgin, intercessor, and saint.

This is how what might be called the traditional female square is composed. The woman is Servant, Seductress, Lover, and Saint.

The striking thing about this abstract yet rich construction is that its active unity is less one isolated term than a pair of terms. Examples abound and have informed most of the literature about women, regardless of whether it was written by men or by women. There is always a woman split between two figures. Thus, the servant, the housewife-mother, is only thinkable if she is combined with the seductress, whose lowest form is the whore. That is why they say that a man can only relate to women in terms of the Mother–Whore dichotomy. But the dangerous seductress is only such to the extent that she is coupled with the female lover's fervor. This is the source of the countless female opposites in literature, where the whole plot depicts the conflict between pure and impure love, desire and love, or the sublime lover confronted with her powerful rival, the loose woman, or the woman of ill repute. But the lover herself borders on the sublime, and if she gives of and sacrifices herself, it may also be in order to lose herself in God through what could be called an upward-leading virginity. It is not for nothing that Goethe ended his sublime *Faust* with the line: "The eternal feminine leads us on high." The truth is, the servant is only a woman because her virtual double is the seductress; the seductress is only powerful because she lands on love's shores; and the lover is only sublime because she comes very close to the female mystic.

But then there's a reverse movement, leading back to the starting point: the sublime female mystic confirms the mother's everyday selflessness, and, as a result, religious and moral prose flows effortlessly from the mystical to the domestic, conveyed by the female figures. The most important of these in our world is obviously the Virgin Mary, sublime to the point of being quasi-divine and at the same time the archetype of the mother, the tender mother of the baby as well as the Mater Dolorosa of the crucified son. The return of the saint's sublimity to the mother's domesticity ultimately changes the square of figures into a circle. By what means does it do so? By the fact that each figure is a figure only insofar as it is in an eccentric relation to another one. So "woman" always means an instance of duality. Even a saintly wife is only so because she was once asked to seduce, she consented to sex, and so she, too, is dangerous, and remains forever so. Otherwise, if she were only innocently and faithfully the domestic wife, why would she have to be locked away, covered up, shielded from other men's gazes? But isn't it this dangerous woman hidden under the veil of the faithful wife who, fired by passion, sneaks away to meet a lover she'd give her life for? And if that lover leaves her, isn't she tempted to devote herself to the saving God in some out-of-the-way convent? But in that case, isn't she the sublime new figure of what the absolutely devoted wife already was, day after day?

In traditional representation, a woman is in one place only insofar as she is also in another. So a woman is that which passes between two places.

But the truth is, the power of the Two is even greater. Indeed, each of the figures is itself split in two.

The simplest example of this is the exchange of women in traditional societies, either the so-called "primitive" ones, which anthropologists used to study, or the ones in our own history. In either case, it's a question of the woman as a higher domestic animal. We know that in some groups a man can only acquire a wife in exchange for a substantial payment, such as two or three cows, some fabrics, etc. In other groups, on the contrary, a man won't marry a woman unless she comes with a substantial payment. This is the dowry system. What explanation is there for the fact that women and money can circulate either in the same direction or in opposite directions? In the case of the dowry, the woman passes from one family to another with a trousseau and money. In the case of pure exchange, the woman passes from one family to another provided that money passes from the beneficiary family to the donor family. The explanation can only be that the acquisition of a girl has two opposite senses, reflected in the two directions in which money circulates. In the first sense, she is a force of labor and reproduction that comes at a high price. In the second, she is of course still a reproductive force but one that has to be taken good care of. This is why the dowry system was, and still is – more or less discreetly – imperative in wealthy milieux, where the woman must show off, display her elegance and culture, and preside at social functions where her clothes must never be inferior to another woman's. That's expensive. An African peasant woman, by contrast, will not just bear children but work hard in the fields. That brings in a little money. Let's say that the acquisition of a wife is suspended between the domestic animal in the sense of labor and the domestic animal in the sense of company and ornamentation. There are some women who are laboring oxen and some who are Persian cats. There are even some – many of them – who try to be both at once.

In other words, the seeming simplicity of the most objective, basic, unequivocally submissive figure of femininity, which is the servant figure, is already eroded from within by two contradictory possibilities.

It could easily be shown that the same is true for the other three. Thus, for example, the figure of the mystic is subjected to the contrasting pressures of a movement of self-abasement, humiliation, and abjection and a movement of glorious ascension. So its image is both a sort of repulsive degradation and a diaphanous light. The Nun is a classic figure of pornography at the same time as she abides, along with Saint Theresa of Ávila, in the light of poetic ecstasy.

We could say that these are just representations, that they're all just male fantasies in origin. That's not wrong as far as the surface content of these representations is concerned. But I will argue that there is a profound, abstract idea in them of what a woman can be. Naturally, we won't be concerned with the anthropological particularity of the figures but rather with the logic of the Two, of the passing-between-two, as the definition of femininity. This femininity is opposed to the strong affirmation of the One, of the single power, that characterizes the traditional male position. Indeed, male logic is summed up in the absolute oneness of the Name-of-the-Father. The symbol of this absolute oneness is, moreover, obvious in the absolute, and absolutely male, oneness of the God of the great monotheisms. Now, it is this One that is critically at stake in the figural in-between place where woman is situated.

We could obviously ask why woman is supposedly the Two of the male One. Just as a joke, we might recall that in France the Social Security code designates men by the number 1 and women by the number 2. My response to this is that this 1 and this 2 have just a plain ordinal value: man is the first sex, woman, the second – "the second sex," as Simone de Beauvoir entitled her book. The One and the Two that I'm talking about have a *cardinal* value: it's a question of internal structure, not hierarchy. I will attempt to show that the formalism dialecticizing the

One and the Two therefore suffices for think-ing sexuation. Or rather – and this is the whole problem we'll end up with – that this formalism *used to* suffice.

Of course, we obviously won't deduce the clas-sic misogynistic accusation of women's duplicity from this female duality that is opposed to the closed nature of the One. But we should keep in mind – and this is the key point – that Woman connotes a process more than a position. What process? That of a passing, precisely. As many poets, and Baudelaire in particular, saw, a woman is first and foremost *une passante*, someone who passes by: "O you whom I might have loved, o you who knew it."

Let's put it more bluntly and say that a woman is that which subverts the One, that which is not a place but an act. I will argue here – and this is a little different from what Lacan says – that it's not the negative relation to the All, the not-All, that governs the formula of sexuation, but rather the relation to the One, precisely insofar as the One is not. You can only understand all this if you're convinced that God is not, and therefore that the One of the Name-of-the-Father is not, either. A woman is the process of this "not-being" that is constitutive of the whole being of the One. This is what has sometimes led people to believe, especially in the romantic metaphysics of love, that a woman is divine. In fact, it's the exact opposite, something that people try to conceal most of the time. A woman is always herself the earthly proof that God doesn't exist, that God doesn't need to exist. All you have to do is look at a woman, really look at her, to be instantly convinced that we can easily do without God. That's why, in traditional societies, women are kept out of sight. This is a much more serious matter than ordinary sexual jealousy. Tradition knows that, to keep God alive no matter what, women absolutely have to be made invisible.

To support this atheistic process by which she asserts the non-being of the One, a woman must constantly create another term that dis-unifies whatever claims to be the One. Thus, she passes between two. It's not that a woman is double or duplicitous, it's that, whenever an attempt is made to assign woman to a place, the Two is the means of going beyond the One of the place via the between-two of that place and its double, its dyadic opposite, which woman's power is able to elicit.

A woman thus creates a double that deposes the One and proudly proclaims its non-being.

In this sense, woman is the going-beyond of the One in the form of a passing-between-Two. That is my speculative definition of the feminine. Note that it is compatible with the traditional circle of the four figures: Servant, Seductress, Lover, and Saint. Traditional oppression simply attempts to enclose the Two's power, its power to subvert the One, within the closed circle of these figures. Tradition is not the destruction of the Two's power. It is its enclosure, in the perhaps mistaken belief that a closed circulation will wear down that power.

So our original problem, that of girls in the contemporary world, is a lot clearer now. We need to examine, with respect to this provisional definition of the feminine, what effects modern prematurity may have, what price has to be paid for the capitalist power that has put an end to the girl in favor of the girl-woman.

Here's what I think about this in a nutshell: very strong pressure is being exerted on the figure of woman from two directions today. The first seeks to unify every woman. The second has to do with childbearing.

Contemporary capitalism is urging, and will eventually require, women to take upon themselves the new form of the One with which it wants to replace the One of symbolic authority, to replace the legitimate, religious authority of the Name-of-the-Father – namely, the One of consumerist, competitive individualism. Boys provide a weak, adolescent, frivolous, lawless, or even a borderline criminal version of this individualism. The girl-woman is being urged to provide a tough, mature, serious, legal, and punitive version of competitive, consumerist individualism. That's why there is a whole bourgeois, authoritarian brand of feminism. It is not calling for a different world to be created but for the world as it is to be turned over to woman power. This feminism demands that women be judges, army generals, bankers, CEOs, Members of Parliament, government ministers, and presidents, and that even for women who aren't any of those things – i.e., almost all women – this be the norm of women's equality and their social value. To that effect, women are regarded as a reserve army for triumphant capitalism.

So, far from being part of the process that creates something different from the One, that creates the Two and the passing-between-Two, a woman becomes the model of the new One, the One that stands boldly and brashly before the competitive market and is both its servant and its master. Contemporary woman will be the symbol of the new One, erected on the ruins of the Name-of-the-Father.

As a result, three of the ancient figures of the feminine – dangerous seduction, the amorous gift, and the mystical sublime – disappear. To be sure, the woman-One is naturally seductive, because seduction is a major weapon of competition. Women bankers and board chairwomen pride themselves on their ability to remain women, precisely in the sense of the seductress. The danger that such seduction represents, however, is one of the One's weapons; it is by no means its double or a threat to it. Seduction is in the service of power. That's why it must not be associated with the self-abandonment of love, which is a weakness and a kind of alienation. The woman-One is free, she's a tough fighter, and if she decides to get into a relationship, it will be based on a contract with mutual benefits. Love becomes the existential form of the contract; it is just one deal among others. And lastly, the woman-One couldn't care less about the mystical sublime. She would much prefer to run real organizations.

Basically, the idea is that not only can women do everything men do, but, under the conditions of capitalism, they can do it better than men. They'll be more realistic than men, more relentless, more tenacious. Why? Precisely because girls no longer have to become the women that they already are, while boys don't know how to become the men that they are not. So the One of individualism is stronger in women than in men.

If we were to indulge in a little science-fiction, perhaps we could simply predict the extinction of the male gender. You'd just have to freeze the sperm of a few tens of millions of men, which would amount to billions of genetic possibilities. Reproduction would thus be guaranteed by artificial insemination. All the males could then be exterminated. And, just as with bees or ants, humanity would only consist of women, who would do everything very well, given that the symbolic order would be minimal, being only the order required by the actual situation of capitalism.

After all, what capitalism requires is a life consisting of work, needs, and satisfactions. An animal life, in short. And it has been proven that what an animal life needs most is females, the males existing only for reproduction. But humanity has perfectly mastered artificial reproduction, without the need for mating or males. So, for the first time in human history, the end of the male gender is a real possibility.

However fictitious this prospect may be, it clearly shows that the crux of it all today is the reproduction of the human race, its modalities and its symbolism. This is the second problem of femininity today. I said that the figures of the Seductress, the Lover, and the Saint were directly threatened with extinction. But what about the figure of woman as a servant? The problem here is that if we admit that women can do everything that men do, the converse, for the time being, is not true. There is one thing that men absolutely can't do, and that's give birth to a baby. Accordingly, the woman remains a servant, naturally not of one man but of the whole human race. If, like men, but for reasons of personal convenience, she declared herself to be incapable of reproducing, incapable of childbearing, then the human race would just have to expect to become extinct. In this sense, for the time being, even the woman-One of capitalism remains a servant: a servant of humanity.

That's why the conversation is so often focused on this one topic today: childbearing, reproduction. These are all the so-called "social" issues that we're constantly hearing about: abortion, infanticide, the responsibility for childcare, sexual consent, homosexual couples, surrogate mothers, and so on. It is also why bourgeois feminism manifests a sort of hostility to motherhood, the last refuge of the old servant figure. This can be seen, for example, in the writings of Élisabeth Badinter,[1] who demands that we put an end to the idea of a "maternal instinct" and affirm that a woman exists fully and completely even if she doesn't have children and doesn't want to have any. That position is perfectly consistent with the contemporary girl-woman, because if a girl is already a woman, the converse is also true: every woman can be a girl, with no desire for children. That may be a completely legitimate option. But you have to admit that it can't be a *rule*, because the problem is, when a rule is formulated, the

1 See *The Conflict: How Modern Motherhood Undermines the Status of Women* (New York: Metropolitan Books, 2012).

consequences of its universalization, as Kant put it, always have to be considered. However, the universalization of the refusal to bear children amounts, quite simply, to the end of the human race. This is such a dim prospect that everyone, of course, ultimately prefers for women to remain the servants of humanity. Once again, this divides the One of the capitalist feminine into a creative duality and thereby raises a very difficult subjective problem for it.

At this point, I feel like saying: let contemporary capitalist societies deal with this problem that *they've* created, after all. My still very unclear view of things is that we've got to both accept the end of the traditional figures and reject the figure of the woman-One as capitalism's reserve army. Women will break out, have already frequently broken out, of the imaginary and symbolic circle made up of the four figures of the Servant, the Seductress, the Lover, and the Saint. But many of them are in no way resigned, on the basis of this negative freedom, to the opposite fate of the woman-One of capital. They know that this contemporary figure destroys the capacity of the Two and replaces it with an abstract unity of servitude. They know that, as a result, childbearing, detached from strong symbolizations, will only subsist as irreducible domestic service, as creativity without any glory. They see that the prospect, even if only a fantasy, of men's extinction would forever make them slaves of themselves and unleash their latent ferocity. What must be affirmed above all, whether you're a man or a woman, is that, to the extent that it exists at all, the woman question cannot be determined by the demands of contemporary capitalist societies. We need to choose a completely external starting point. And this is probably why, for the first time, there's no escaping the fact that the feminine, as newly clarified, is linked to a philosophical gesture. Because the new starting point can be neither biological nor social nor legal. It can only be a gesture of thought linked to the creation of symbols. A gesture linked, therefore, to the adventures of philosophy, and one that is all the newer given that this female creation of symbols will have to include childbearing in a dimension different from reproductive animality.

Let's assume that the order of symbol creation, or the order of the Law, is no longer absolutely dependent on the Name-of-the-Father. We then have a thinking of truths free of all transcendence. God is really dead. And since God is dead, the absolute One of male closure can no longer govern the entire order of symbolic and philosophical thinking. A sexuation of this thinking is inevitable. How, then, does this sexuation function in the real domains of these truths without God, without paternal guarantee? These are the questions we need to begin with. Concretely: what is a woman who engages in the politics of emancipation? What is a woman artist, musician, painter, or poet? A woman who is brilliant in math or physics? A woman who, rather than being some mysterious goddess, takes equal responsibility for thought and action in a love relationship? What is a woman philosopher? And, conversely, what do creative politics, poetry, music, cinema, mathematics, or love become – what does philosophy become – once the word "woman" resonates in them in tune with the power of symbol-creating equality?

These questions are being worked on, because women are working on them, in a new in-between place that can be described as: neither Tradition nor the dominant Contemporary. Women will pass between the two and subvert the One that they are being urged to become. This is a unique tension. Indeed, women should be much more wary today of what capitalism is offering them in the way of liberation than they should be of men. I don't know what women will invent, given the predicament they're in. But I trust them absolutely. What I'm sure of, without really knowing why, is that they'll invent a new girl. She will be the girl who is determined to become the new woman, the woman that women are not and must become, the woman who is fully involved in the creation of symbols and will also include childbearing in it. The woman who will thereby induce men to share fully in all the consequences, henceforth universally symbolized, of reproduction. So childbearing and childcare will never again mean being a servant. Men and women will share in a new universal symbolization of birth and all its consequences. This girl, as yet unknown but who is coming, will be able to proclaim, is probably already proclaiming somewhere, to the sky empty of God:

Beautiful heaven, true heaven, look how I change![2]

2 Paul Valéry, "The Graveyard by the Sea," tr. C. Day Lewis, in *Selected Writings of Paul Valéry* (New York: New Directions, 1964), 43.